At Home with Science

Counting Sheep!

Why do we sleep?

Written by Janice Lobb

Illustrated by Peter Utton and Ann Savage

KINGFISHER

NEW YORK

KINGFISHER
Larousse Kingfisher Chambers Inc.
80 Maiden Lane
New York, New York 10038
www.kingfisherpub.com

First published in 2001
10 9 8 7 6 5 4 3 2 1

1TR/0501/FR/SC/128JDA

Created and designed by Snapdragon Publishing Ltd.

Copyright © Snapdragon Publishing Ltd. 2001

All rights reserved under International and Pan-American
Copyright Conventions

LIBRARY OF CONGRESS CATALOGING-IN-PUBLICATION DATA
has been applied for.

ISBN 0-7534-5361-4

Printed in Hong Kong

For Snapdragon
Editorial Director Jackie Fortey
Art Director Chris Legee
Designers Chris Legee and Joy Fitzsimons

For Kingfisher
Editors Jennie Morris and Emma Wild
Series Art Editor Mike Davis
DTP Manager Nicky Studdart
Production Controller Debbie Otter

Contents

About this book

Have you ever asked why you have to go to bed or how the moon gets its light, or wondered why your hair sometimes sticks out straight when you brush it? This book is about the science that happens every day in your bedroom. Look around, and you'll soon be making your own discoveries!

Hall of Fame

Archie and his friends are here to help you. They are each named after a famous scientist—apart from Bob the (rubber) duck, who is a young scientist like you!

Archie
ARCHIMEDES (287–212 B.C.) The Greek scientist Archimedes figured out why things float or sink while he was in the bathtub. According to the story, he was so pleased that he leaped up, shouting "Eureka!" which means "I've done it!"

Frank
BENJAMIN FRANKLIN (1706–1790) Besides being one of the most important figures in American history, he was also a noted scientist. In a dangerous experiment in which he flew a kite in a storm, he proved that lightning is actually electricity.

Marie
MARIE CURIE (1867–1934) Girls did not go to college in Poland, where Marie Curie grew up, so she went to Paris to study. Later, she worked on radioactivity and received two Nobel prizes for her discoveries, in 1903 and 1911.

Dot
DOROTHY HODGKIN (1910–1994) Dorothy Hodgkin was a British scientist who made many important discoveries about molecules and atoms, the tiny particles that make up everything around us. She was given the Nobel prize for Chemistry in 1964.

See for yourself!

1 Read about the science in your bedroom, then try the "See for yourself!" experiments to discover how it works. In science, experiments are used to find or show the answers.

Ow-ooo!

Whoo! Whoo!

2 Carefully read the instructions for each experiment, making sure you follow the numbered steps in the correct order.

Crunch!

Twang!

3 Here are some of the things you will need. Have everything ready before you start each experiment.

Fabric scraps

Double-sided tape

Plastic bottle

Jar lids

Plastic straws

Spoon

Ball

Tinfoil ball

Scissors

Scented oils

Mug

Thread

Tacks

Button

Silver coin

4 # Safety first!

Some scientists took risks to make their discoveries, but our experiments are safe. Just make sure that you tell an adult what you are doing, and get their help when you see the red warning button.

Amazing facts

WOW!

You'll notice that some words are written in *italics*. You can learn more about them in the glossary at the back of the book. And if you want to find out some amazing facts, keep an eye out for the "Wow!" panels.

Keep an eye out for useful tips!

Have fun!

Why do I have to go to bed?

When you are awake, your brain—the part of your body that controls what you do—receives information from your *senses*. They tell it about everything you see, hear, taste, smell, and feel. Your brain needs time to figure this out and sort the information, which it does when you are asleep. Dreaming is part of this sorting process. The brain stores most memories, but lets you forget things that you don't need. If you don't get enough sleep, you can become forgetful or even sick.

When is the best time to go to bed?

When the bed won't come to you!

Sweet dreams!

There are things that you do all the time without thinking, such as breathing. This happens even while you are asleep. Part of your brain keeps you alive without you having to think about it.

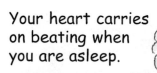

Your heart carries on beating when you are asleep.

Brain

Dream

Even when you are asleep, your brain sends messages to your breathing muscles.

Children grow more when they are asleep than when they are awake.

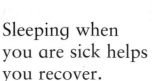

Sleeping when you are sick helps you recover.

Plenty of "beauty sleep" gives your skin a chance to repair itself.

See for yourself!

1 Try to learn a short poem before you go to bed. Can you remember it in the morning?

2 Try learning another poem when you get up. Can you remember it when you go to bed? When is the best time to learn new things?

3 If you remember your dreams when you wake up, try to write them down. You will usually forget them quickly if you don't.

In his dream Archie is dancing with Bob. What do you dream about?

Sleeping beauty

WOW!

On average, a person spends 23 years of their life asleep—but not usually all at once!

Try to sleep at the right times!

7

Why do I have bedding?

The sheet, blankets, pillows, and mattress on your bed help make you comfortable while you sleep. If the air around you is cold, you lose *heat* by *convection*. This means that as the air next to your body warms up, it moves away and takes heat with it. Your comforter or blanket stops this from happening by acting as *insulation*. The warm air is trapped and cannot escape. In hot weather, when you are already warm, you probably need thinner sheets.

Should I tell you the joke about the bed?

It hasn't been made yet!

Saving heat

Animals and birds have thick fur and feathers. They make nests of insulating materials to help their babies stay warm.

Feather-filled comforter

We use similar materials in comforters and blankets to trap warm air and to keep it close to our bodies. Mattresses are softer and warmer than the cold, hard ground.

Insulation can keep heat out as well as in. Picnic food will stay cool in a padded bag.

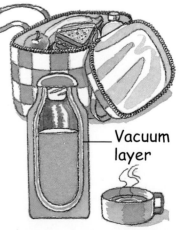

Vacuum layer

A *vacuum* thermos can keep drinks hot or cold.

8

See for yourself! ✋

1 Collect scraps of different fabrics, such as a cotton dishcloth, a wool sweater, a silk scarf, and furry material.

Furry material

Cotton dishcloth

Silk scarf

Wool sweater

2 Now see how well they act as insulation. Ask a grown-up to fill some plastic bottles with water hot to the touch.

Caps on

3 Wrap each bottle, except for one, in a piece of material. Leave them to cool in the same place.

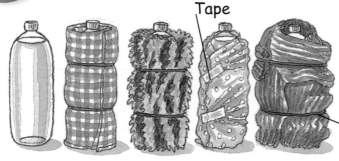

Tape

Rubber band

4 After about 30 minutes, feel the bottles. Are any of them still warm? Put them in order by temperature. Which material was the best insulator?

Which material would make the best cover for Archie's hot-water bottle?

Don't forget to make your bed!

WOW!

Hair

Llama

Hollow hairs

Most mammals and birds have air trapped between their hair or feathers to help them stay warm. Llamas have hollow hairs that give them even more insulation.

Why does my clock tick?

Your bedroom clock tells you when it is time to get up. Long ago, people rose when the sun rose and measured hours using silent sand timers. Your clock works day and night, showing hours and minutes. A *digital* clock is silent. A clock makes a ticking noise if it has moving parts called clockwork. Clockwork is made up of gearwheels, which are turned by *energy* stored in a battery or a wound-up spring. The clock "ticks" as the gearwheels click around. The clock stops when it needs to be wound up, or it needs a new battery.

What do you do with a sick clock?

Nothing. It will get better with time!

How clocks work

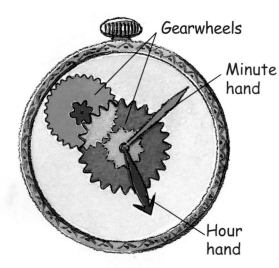

Gearwheels

Minute hand

Hour hand

The gearwheels inside a clock turn the big (minute) hand and the little (hour) hand at different speeds, so we can tell the time.

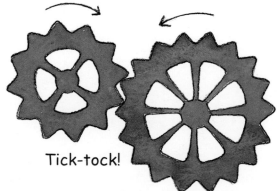

One wheel goes one way, and the other goes the opposite way.

Tick-tock!

A gearwheel is a wheel with teeth around its edge. The teeth on one wheel catch on the next and help it turn around.

Instead of a face and hands, a digital clock has a *liquid crystal display* (LCD) that just shows numbers.

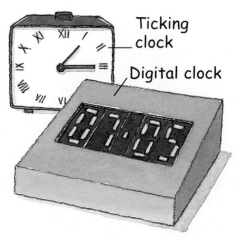

Ticking clock

Digital clock

See for yourself!

1 To make a gearwheel, carefully cut up some plastic straws. Use double-sided tape to stick ten pieces around the top of a large jar lid.

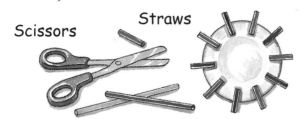

Scissors

Straws

2 Using a smaller lid, make another gearwheel with eight teeth. These are your model gearwheels.

Eight teeth

Ten teeth

3 Ask a grown-up to stick a tack in the middle of the underside of each gearwheel. This will help your gearwheels turn.

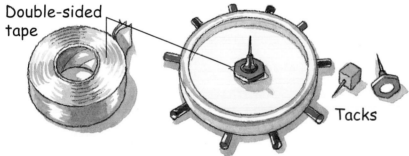

Double-sided tape

Tacks

4 Push the tacks into a cardboard box, so that when the gearwheels turn, the teeth catch on each other. Turn the big wheel, and watch it turn the little wheel.

Perfect time

WOW!

The most accurate clock is an atomic clock, which loses less than one second in three million years. A quartz crystal, like the ones in digital watches, is made to *vibrate* using a special metal called caesium. One second is the time taken for 9,192,631,770 vibrations, which is incredibly fast.

Practice telling time!

Why does my hair stick out straight?

What did the brush say to the hair?

I'll have to charge you for this!

Is it sometimes impossible to get your hair to lie flat when you brush it? Does it stick out straight when you comb it? This problem is caused by *static electricity*. When you use a plastic brush or comb, you remove tiny electrical *particles* called *electrons* from your hair. This leaves the outside of each hair *electrically charged*. Because the charge on each hair is the same, the electricity pushes the hairs away from each other, so the hairs fluff out instead of lying flat together.

Electrical charges

Magnets will push each other away like electrically charged hairs. If you try to move the same ends, or *poles*, of two magnets together, they repel, or push each other away. North (N) will repel north, and south (S) will repel south.

Walking in socks on a thick carpet can charge your whole body. If you touch a metal doorknob, you may get a surprise jolt from a little electric shock!

Static electricity can also attract objects. It attracts dust to glass windows and TV screens.

Charges that are different pull toward, or attract, each other.

12

See for yourself!

1 Mix some coarse salt or sugar with finely-ground pepper or talcum powder. Sprinkle the mixture on a flat surface.

2 Rub a plastic spoon or ruler with a wool cloth or the sleeve of your sweater to charge it with static electricity.

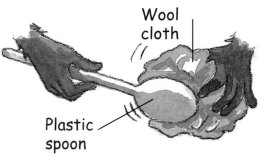

Wool cloth

Plastic spoon

3 Hold the spoon over the mixture and gradually lower it. The fine powder or pepper will jump up to the spoon and stick to it.

Fine powder

4 If you hold the spoon even lower, some of the salt or sugar will jump up too. Static electricity makes this happen.

Salt and sugar are heavier than fine powder.

Charged clouds

WOW!

Electrical charges

In thunderstorms, swirling ice particles in clouds rub together and become charged with static electricity. This produces lightning. Huge sparks of *electricity* jump through the air and can travel between clouds or down to the ground.

Rub a balloon against your sweater to charge it with static electricity.

How does my light work?

Why do you have a book about lamps?

For a little light reading!

When things become *white-hot*, they send out some of their energy as *light*. The energy in a candle comes from the burning wax. The candle gets shorter as the wax is used up. When you turn on an electric light, the bulb lights up. Unlike a candle, the bulb is not used up, because it does not burn. The energy it uses is electricity, which travels to the bulb through wires for as long as the light is switched on.

How light travels

Inside a glass lightbulb there is a fine metal wire called the *filament*. When electricity flows through the filament, it becomes white-hot and gives off light.

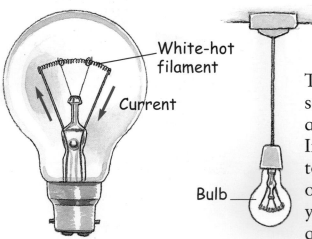

White-hot filament

Current

Bulb

The light is sent out in all directions. If you want it to go in only one direction, you must use a lampshade.

The lampshade directs light onto the wall.

Opaque object

Light always travels in straight lines, so it cannot go around corners. When light reaches an *opaque* object that blocks its way, it casts a shadow.

See for yourself!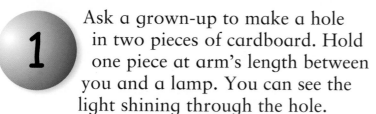

1 Ask a grown-up to make a hole in two pieces of cardboard. Hold one piece at arm's length between you and a lamp. You can see the light shining through the hole.

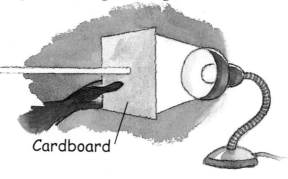

Cardboard

2 Hold the second piece of cardboard between you and the first piece. You can only see the light if the two holes are lined up.

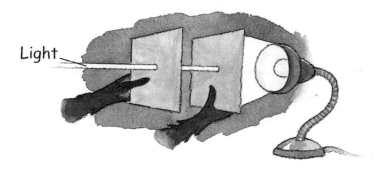

Light

3 Let the lamp shine on a wall. Use your hands or cut out a puppet to put between the lamp and the wall. Have fun making shadow pictures.

Is this a butterfly or a bird?

Bright idea!

WOW!

The famous inventor Thomas Edison made the first electric lightbulb in 1879. It contained a filament made of carbon, which glowed when an electric current passed through it. People soon began to replace gas lamps in their homes with electric lights.

Don't touch! It might still be hot!

What's in my closet?

Humans wear clothes because, unlike other animals, we often need extra protection against the weather. When it is hot, lightweight clothes allow heat to escape from our skin and protect us from the sun. Lighter colors, such as white, also *reflect* sunlight and help keep us cool. In cold weather we wear warmer and heavier clothes that trap air and keep in heat. People who make clothes dye materials in many colors. We can wear our favorite colors and create a look different from everyone else.

> What sits in your closet with its tongue hanging out?

> Your shoe!

Fibers and dyes

Clothes are made from *fibers*. Some fibers are natural (from plants or animals). Cotton comes from plants; wool comes from animals.

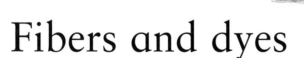

Seed pod with fibers inside

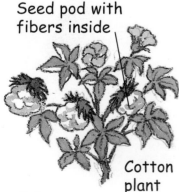

Cotton plant

Wool

Jacob sheep

Some fibers have several natural colors. Jacob sheep, for example, have several shades in their wool.

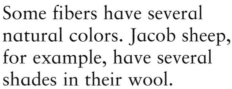

Liquid chemicals

Fibers

Thread

Liquid chemicals are squirted through holes in a machine to make *synthetic* fibers.

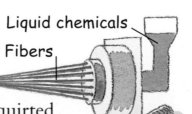

Dye

Coal

Most of the *dyes* used to color clothes are made from oil or coal. There are thousands of different colors to choose from.

16

See for yourself!

1 How many ways can you sort your clothes? Look at the labels to help you decide. Which ones contain synthetic fibers? Polyester, nylon, and acrylic are examples of synthetic fibers.

2 Which clothes are for cold weather? If they trap air, because they are fluffy or padded, they keep heat in. Thin clothes are better for warmer weather.

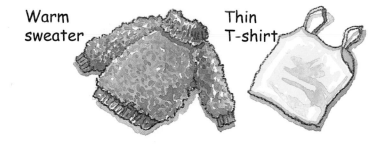

Warm sweater

Thin T-shirt

3 Do you have a favorite color? If you sort your clothes into different colors, is there one pile that is larger than all the rest?

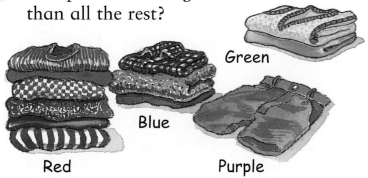

Green

Blue

Red

Purple

North Pole

Arctic hare with summer coat

Arctic hare with winter coat

Seasonal styles!

There are animals, such as the arctic hare and the snow mouse, that have a different coat for each season. The arctic hare is grayish-brown in the summer, but in the winter it turns white to blend in with the snow. This helps it hide from its enemies. Near the North Pole, where there is always snow, it stays white throughout the year.

Fold and hang up your clothes!

Why does perfume smell nice?

An elephant's trunk!

What's long, gray, and smells?

You smell things when tiny particles drift through the air and up into your nose. Special scent detectors catch the particles and send messages to your brain. The sense of smell helps us enjoy the food we eat. We also enjoy smells for their own sake, like the scents that many flowers use to attract insects. There are smelly chemicals in other parts of plants too. They are extracted from plants as *essential oils* and used to make perfumes.

How smells travel

Essential oils *evaporate* so their smell travels through the air. We cannot smell things that don't evaporate (turn into vapor).

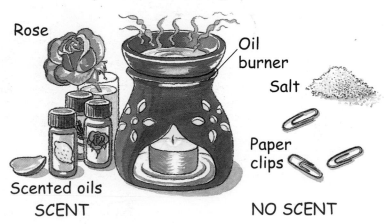

Scented liquids turn into vapor. Vapor travels through the air.

Rose

Oil burner

Salt

Scented oils

SCENT

Paper clips

NO SCENT

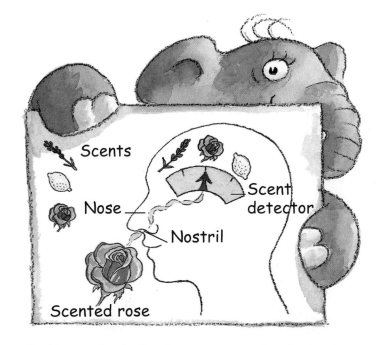

Scents

Scent detector

Nose

Nostril

Scented rose

When you breathe in, scents travel up your nose. Each scent has particles of a different size and shape. Scent detectors in your nose can tell the difference between them.

See for yourself!

1 Put some water in two saucers. Put one on top of a radiator or on a sunny windowsill. Put the other on a plate of ice cubes in a shady area.

Water

Ice

Water

2 Ask a grown-up to help you add a few drops of scented oil, such as lavender, to each saucer, and wait a little while.

Scented oil

Water

Ice

Water and scented oil

3 Then walk around sniffing. Which one can you smell first? Which smells stronger? Warmth should help the smells escape into the air.

Water and scented oil

Escaping vapor

Good scents!

WOW!

Mmm!

Smells can have an effect on our brains, although we may not notice. Some scents, such as lavender and camomile, help us relax. Others, including lemon and tea tree, help us wake up.

Be careful with scented oils—they may smell very strong.

19

What lives in my bedroom?

What did one bedbug say to the other?

Let's grab a bite!

Some insects and bugs find your bedroom just as cozy as you do. Spiders walk up walls and drainpipes. Climbing plants and window boxes help them find their way in. At night moths, june bugs, and crane flies come in through open windows, attracted by the light. Most of these small visitors are harmless, but fleas, which hitch a ride on pets, and mosquitoes are out looking for blood. In the fall ladybugs and butterflies may arrive, looking for somewhere to *hibernate*.

What is an insect?

June bugs, moths, and butterflies are flying insects. They have six legs and large feelers called antennae. Fleas are insects too, but they don't have wings.

Spiders and mites are not insects—they are *arachnids*. They cannot fly and have eight legs. Slugs and snails have soft bodies and no legs at all. They are called *mollusks*.

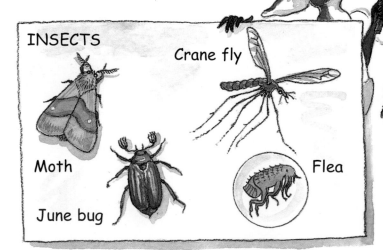

INSECTS

Crane fly

Moth

June bug

Flea

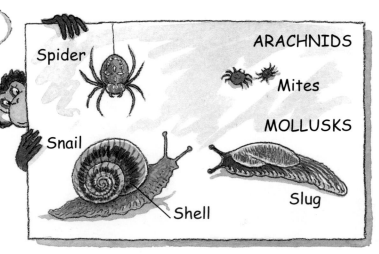

Spider

ARACHNIDS

Mites

MOLLUSKS

Snail

Shell

Slug

See for yourself! ✋

1 What can you hear when it is quiet at night? You might hear the buzz of a fly or the whine of a mosquito.

Mosquito

2 In the winter take a peek in the folds of your curtains. You may find a sleeping ladybug or butterfly. Do not disturb it. It will wake up and fly away in the spring.

Butterfly · Ladybug

3 Look for the slimy trails of slugs and snails that have wandered inside during the night.

Snail

Snail trail

Sneezy bugs

WOW!

Achooo!

The tiniest uninvited guests are dust mites, which live in household dust. They feed on mold growing on anything slightly damp, including your bedding. People can sometimes be allergic to them. They can make us sneeze and wheeze.

Dust mite

Don't touch bugs that bite or sting!

Why do we close the curtains?

It is easier to sleep in the dark because when your eyes are open, they keep your brain busy by sending it messages. When you close your eyes to go to sleep, there is nothing to look at, and you aren't tempted to open them again. Most houses and apartments have windows made of colorless glass that let in a lot of light. Covering them with curtains or blinds keeps out the light while you are sleeping. You will not be disturbed by streetlights, moonlight, the headlights of passing cars, or by the sun when it rises in the morning.

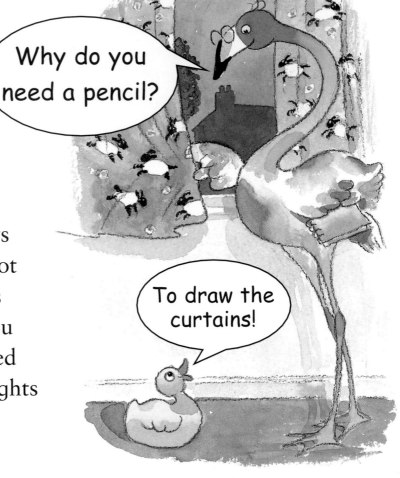

Why do you need a pencil?

To draw the curtains!

Light and materials

Something that is *transparent* lets light through it. You can see what is on the other side. Opaque materials hold back all the light. You can't see through them at all.

Light can't go through a blindfold.

Light can go through glasses.

Not all glass is colorless. Some glass can let through only one color, some is dark, and some looks milky or pearly.

Dark glass

Colored glass

Pearly glass

See for yourself!

1 Find a nice, bright sunbeam or shine a desk lamp on a wall. The light shining on the wall has traveled through air, which is transparent and colorless.

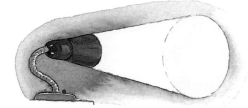

2 Look through a clear piece of plastic or plastic wrap. You can see what is on the other side because it is transparent. Hold it in the light beam. There is almost no shadow.

Faint shadow of edge

3 Hold a thick piece of cardboard up to the light. You can't see anything through it because it is opaque. Hold it in the light beam. It casts a dark shadow.

Dark shadow

4 Hold up other objects, such as drinking glasses, candy wrappers, and colored plastic. How much light goes through them? What kind of light can you see?

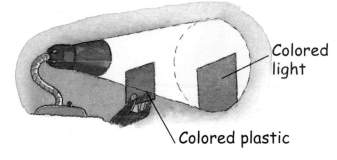

Colored light

Colored plastic

What's cooking?

Several thousand years ago someone heated a mixture of sand, ashes, and limestone until it was red-hot and runny. They had discovered the "recipe" for glass!

WOW!

Hot furnace

Sand

Glass

Lime

Ash

Always handle glass objects very carefully.

Why can nighttime seem scary?

What's a ghost's favorite game?

Hide and shriek!

Have strange nighttime noises ever made you hide under your covers? Don't worry—there is a reason you hear different noises at night. Sounds are made when something moves and causes vibrations in the air, which our ears pick up. Because it is quieter at nighttime, we frequently hear noises that are hard to hear during the day, such as the creaking of a house. We also hear sounds of nighttime animals that can seem eerie and spooky. If we hear a sound or see a shadowy shape in the dark, we try to imagine what it is, but we don't always get it right!

Spooky sounds

Wood floorboards expand (get longer) in the heat of the day, then contract (get shorter) as they cool down at night. They creak as they move.

Owls hoot

Mice squeak

Wood creaks as it moves.

Sound travels farther at night. A layer of warm air above the cold night air reflects sound like a mirror reflects light.

Air still warm from the day

Reflected sound

Dogs bark

Cats meow

Air near the ground cools when the sun sets.

See for yourself!

1 Can you make your own spooky nighttime noises? Try howling like a dog or hooting like an owl.

Ow-oooo!

Whoo! Whoo!

2 See what creepy, creaky noises you can make by bending things or rubbing things together. Think how you might do the sound effects for a play about a haunted house.

Crunch!

Twang!

3 Some things can look scary in the dark. Does anything in your room, like a bathrobe, make a spooky shape?

Super-hearing!

WOW!

Bats make high-pitched squeaks.

Children have more sensitive ears than adults and often hear higher sounds. They can sometimes even pick up the *ultrasonic* sounds made by bats. So it is not surprising they hear strange noises!

There's no reason to be afraid of the dark.

How does a cradle rock?

When a cradle stands still on its rockers, it is *balanced*—we say it is in *equilibrium*. If you give the cradle a push from one side, this acts as a *force* that upsets the equilibrium. The cradle tries to rock back to its starting position, but it moves too fast and goes too far in the opposite direction. Each rock is smaller than the last, so the cradle slows down and finally comes to a stop where it started. To keep the cradle rocking, you have to give it another push as it slows down.

What does a cradle do to music?

Rock and roll!

Keeping a balance

When the cradle is still, it is balanced. *Gravity* pulls down on one side as much as it does on the other.

Both sides are equal

Gravity pulls this side down . . .

. . . as much as this one.

Balance point is in the middle

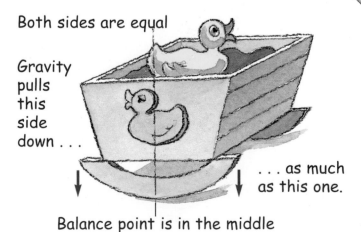

Gravity pulls down more on this side.

Old balance point

New balance point

When it is pushed out of position, there is more of the cradle on one side of the balance point than the other.

As the cradle rocks, it moves back and forth until both sides are balanced again.

See for yourself!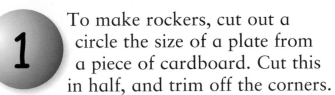

1 To make rockers, cut out a circle the size of a plate from a piece of cardboard. Cut this in half, and trim off the corners.

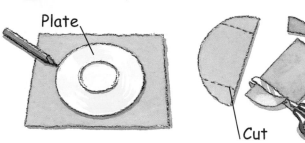

Plate

Cut

2 To make your cradle, tape or glue a rocker to each end of a child's shoebox.

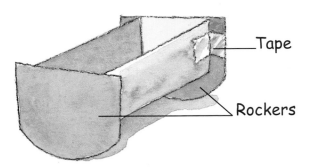

Tape

Rockers

3 Hang a button on a thread down the middle of one rocker. Make a mark on the cardboard halfway down, under the thread.

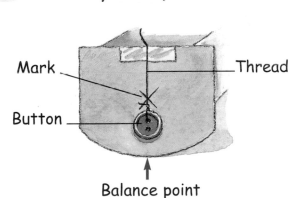

Mark

Button

Thread

Balance point

4 Tilt your cradle. On which side of the thread is the mark? When you let go, it will always rock in the direction of the mark.

Cradle rocks back this way

Cradle rocks back this way

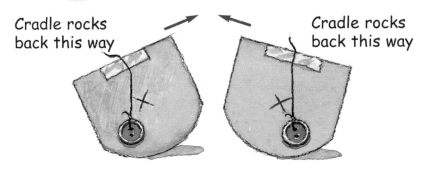

Going green!

Gentle rocking can help you fall asleep. However, too much rocking can make you feel queasy. It upsets the part of your inner ear that helps you keep your balance.

WOW!

Some animals like swinging too!

What is moonlight?

The sun gives off energy in the form of heat and light, which travel through space. Some of it reaches Earth, giving us bright, hot sunshine; some of it hits the moon before bouncing to Earth. This reflected sunlight is called moonlight. Because moonlight has to travel farther than sunlight before reaching Earth, it is dimmer and cooler than sunlight. As the moon goes around Earth, the amount of reflected light we see changes.

Why isn't the moon hungry?

Because it's full!

The changing light of the moon

FULL MOON

Moon

Earth

Night | Day

Sun

Full moon shines on the dark side of Earth.

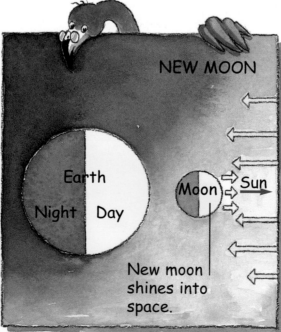

NEW MOON

Earth

Night | Day

Moon

Sun

New moon shines into space.

The most moonlight is seen during a full moon, when the moon looks like a complete circle. As the moon continues to go around Earth, only part of the light is reflected back to Earth. When there is a new moon, we do not get any reflected light, and we cannot see the moon from Earth at night.

See for yourself!

1 Put a ball in the top of a mug. This is Earth. Attach a sticker to the side and shine a light on it. This is the sun shining on you (the sticker) during the day.

This side is in shadow. It is night on this side.

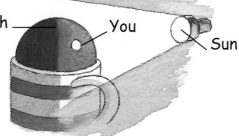

2 Turn Earth around until the sticker is on the edge of the shadow. This is sunset. Now turn it until you are in nighttime.

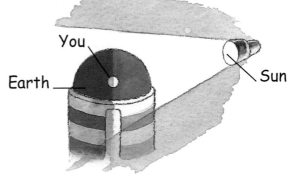

3 Tape a shiny silver coin or tinfoil ball to the end of a pencil. Hold it behind Earth, so that it reflects the sun's light onto the sticker. This is a full moon.

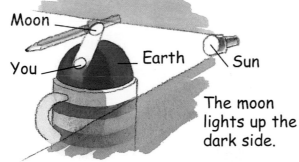

The moon lights up the dark side.

4 Move the moon around and try to reflect light onto the sticker. You will find that no other position gives out so much moonlight.

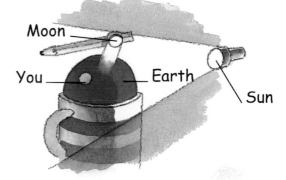

Earthshine

WOW!

Look for a moon shadow!

If you were on the moon, you would see light reflected from Earth—called earthshine. When Earth has a new moon, the moon has a "full Earth," and when Earth has a full moon, the moon has a "new Earth."

Bedroom quiz

1 How does your comforter keep you warm?
    a) It traps cold air
    b) It traps warm air
    c) It traps sunlight

2 What makes a ticking clock keep time?
    a) Candles
    b) Sand
    c) Gearwheels

3 What sometimes happens to your hair when you brush it?
    a) It sticks out straight
    b) It changes color
    c) It stops growing

4 What makes a lightbulb give off light?
    a) Gravity
    b) Energy
    c) Friction

5 What type of animal does wool come from?
    a) A cow
    b) A horse
    c) A sheep

6 What kind of animal is a butterfly?
    a) An insect
    b) An arachnid
    c) A mollusk

7 Where are your scent detectors?
    a) In your nose
    b) In your ears
    c) In your throat

8 What type of material is glass?
    a) Transparent
    b) Stretchy
    c) Spongy

9 How do sounds reach us through the air?
    a) As vibrations
    b) As light rays
    c) As shadows

10 What makes the light reflected by the moon?
    a) The stars
    b) The sun
    c) The earth

Answers on page 32

Glossary

Arachnids
Small, wingless animals with eight jointed legs and bodies that are in two sections.

Balanced
When forces that could cause movement in one direction are canceled out by equal forces in the opposite direction.

Convection
The movement of heat through a liquid or gas. The heat is carried by currents of heated particles.

Digital
Showing an amount or time as a series of numbers, or digits, like on a digital clock.

Dyes
Substances that stick to cloth fibers and color them.

Electrically charged
A surface that is electrically charged has too many—or too few—electrons.

Electricity
A type of energy carried along by electrically charged particles.

Electron
A tiny particle that carries electrical energy.

Energy
The ability to do work or take action.

Equilibrium
A state in which things are balanced.

Essential oils
Perfumed, oily substances produced by some plants.

Evaporate
To change from a visible liquid into an invisible vapor, without being hot enough to boil.

Fibers
Long, thin, flexible, threadlike structures.

Filament
The thin metal wire in a lightbulb, which becomes white-hot without melting.

Force
A push or pull that changes something's movement or shape.

Gravity
Earth's downward pull, which makes things fall.

Heat
A type of energy that warms things up, making them expand, evaporate, melt, or boil.

Hibernate
To spend the winter in a deep sleep, avoiding the cold and lack of food.

Insulation
Material used to slow down or stop the movement of heat.

Light
The energy given off by white-hot objects that lets us see things.

Liquid crystal display (LCD) An electronic display of numbers and letters made of liquid crystals between two sheets of glass or plastic.

Mollusks
Animals without a backbone and with bodies made of muscle; some have shells.

Opaque
When something does not allow light to pass through it.

Particles
Very small parts or pieces of something.

Poles
The two ends of a magnet. When the magnet is free to move, the ends point toward Earth's north and south poles.

Reflect
To bounce light, heat, or sound off a surface.

Senses
Parts of the nervous system (the network of cells that takes messages around the body) that tell the body what is happening to it.

Static electricity
Electrical energy that stays in one place, instead of flowing as a current.

Synthetic
Man-made, not natural.

Transparent
A material or substance you can see through.

Ultrasonic
Vibrations that are too fast for an adult human ear to detect as sound.

Vacuum
A space from which the air has been taken out.

Vibrate
To move back and forth quickly.

White-hot
When something gets so hot that it can't keep all its energy in, so it gives out white light as well as heat.

Index

Answers to Bedroom quiz on page 30
1 b **2** c **3** a **4** b **5** c **6** a **7** a **8** a **9** a **10** b